Flav...

LEICEST...
& RU...LD

RECIPES

Compiled by Julia Skinner

THE FRANCIS FRITH COLLECTION

www.francisfrith.com

First published in the United Kingdom in 2012 by The Francis Frith Collection®

This edition published exclusively for Bradwell Books in 2012
For trade enquiries see: www.bradwellbooks.com or tel: 0800 834 920
ISBN 978-1-84589-692-8

British Library Cataloguing in Publication Data

Flavours of Leicestershire and Rutland - Recipes
Compiled by Julia Skinner

The Francis Frith Collection
Oakley Business Park,
Wylye Road, Dinton,
Wiltshire SP3 5EU
Tel: +44 (0) 1722 716 376
Email: info@francisfrith.co.uk

www.francisfrith.com

Printed and bound in Malaysia
Contains material sourced from responsibly managed forests

Front Cover: **FOXTON, GRAND UNION CANAL c1960** F159004p
Frontispiece: **BITTESWELL, THE VILLAGE c1955** B584016
Contents: **LOUGHBOROUGH, HIGH STREET c1955** L197003

The colour-tinting is for illustrative purposes only, and is not intended to be historically accurate

CONTENTS

2   Soups and Snacks

10   Cheese and Vegetable Dishes

20   Fish

22   Meat

42   Puddings

44   Teatime and Baking

54   Francis Frith - Pioneer Victorian Photographer

'Bean-belly Leicestershire' was once a name given to the county because of the extent to which beans were grown there, particularly broad beans, which were grown in abundance in Leicestershire in the past. There was an old saying 'Shake a Leicestershire yeoman, and you will hear the beans rattle in his belly', a reference to beans forming the staple diet of the county's agricultural labourers in former times. This fact is reflected in the name of the hamlet of Barton in the Beans, near Hinckley, which would once have been surrounded by beanfields, humming with happy bees when the plants were in flower.

QUENIBOROUGH, THE VILLAGE AND ST MARY'S CHURCH c1955
Q12001

RECIPE

BEAN AND BACON BROTH

This recipe uses fresh peas and fresh broad beans, which are in season from late May to August, but you can use frozen peas and beans to make this broth out of season. If using early season broad beans that are small and tender, use them as they are; if using later season fresh beans (about the size of a 10p piece or larger), remove the outer skin of the beans before use.

225g/8oz shelled weight of fresh broad beans
225g/8oz shelled weight of fresh peas
1 large onion, peeled and roughly chopped
450ml/ ¾ pint milk
300ml/ ½ pint vegetable or chicken stock
Salt and pepper to taste
2 rashers bacon, de-rinded, grilled and chopped into
  small pieces to garnish
Fresh parsley, finely chopped, to garnish

Place the broad beans, peas, chopped onion, milk and stock in a large saucepan. Bring to a gentle boil, then reduce the heat and simmer gently for about 20 minutes until the beans are tender, or a little longer if using later season beans.

When the beans are tender, remove the pan from the heat and allow the broth to cool a little. Purée half the broth in a blender or liquidiser, then return the mixture to the remaining broth in the pan. Season to taste, then reheat gently and serve the broth garnished with the bacon pieces and a little chopped fresh parsley.

RECIPE

BROAD BEAN SPREAD

Broad beans are in season from late May to August, and are best eaten as young as possible, when they are very tender. A nice way of serving young broad beans, about the size of a thumbnail, is to cook them in boiling water for about 5 minutes, drain and allow them to cool, then roll them in a cold dressing of crème fraiche, chopped fresh chives, finely chopped garlic and freshly ground black pepper.

Slightly older beans (about the size of a 10p piece) will need to have their outer coating removed, and then cooked for around 5-8 minutes until they are tender, and later in the season, the larger, tougher beans need a longer cooking time. This recipe for a broad bean hummous-style spread is an excellent way of using older beans and comes out a wonderful shade of green!

> 450g/1 lb shelled weight fresh broad beans
> 1 clove of garlic, crushed
> 4-5 tablespoonfuls good olive oil
> Juice of half a lemon (perhaps a little more if needed)
> Salt and freshly ground black pepper to taste

Pop the beans out of their outer skins, then cook them in boiling water until they are tender (see above), then drain. Blitz the beans in a blender with a crushed clove of garlic, some freshly ground black pepper, 4 tablespoonfuls of olive oil, the juice of about half a lemon (to taste) and salt to taste, if needed. If the mixture is too thick, add more oil and lemon juice until the required consistency is reached.

This spread is particularly good with oatcakes.

SYSTON, THE GREEN c1955 S488010

STILTON CHEESE

Stilton cheese was first developed in the villages to the east of Melton Mowbray, possibly as early as the 14th century. The cheese became famous in the early 18th century when Mrs Frances Pawlett, a dairywoman who lived near Melton Mowbray, entered into a business arrangement with her brother-in-law Cooper Thornhill, who agreed to market her cheese. Mr Thornhill was the owner of the Bell Inn at Stilton (then in Huntingdonshire but now in Cambridgeshire), a coaching inn and staging post along what is now the A1 between London and York. He began to introduce the cheese to travellers staying at the inn and it became popular, making Stilton a town 'famous for cheese', as Daniel Defoe recorded in the 1720s. So it was that the cheese took its name from the town where it was sold and distributed from, rather than where it was made – Stilton cheese has never actually been made in Stilton. By the end of the 18th century Stilton cheese was being made in great quantities around Melton Mowbray and in many Rutland villages.

Stilton, 'The King of Cheeses', is a creamy blue-veined cheese with an excellent flavour and a texture that softens as it blues and mellows. A 16 lb Stilton cheese takes 17 gallons of milk to produce, and at least two months to mature. By the early 20th century the making of Stilton cheese had extended to the neighbouring areas of Nottinghamshire and Derbyshire. The Stilton cheese-makers then defined their product and sought legal protection for it to prevent the development of inferior imitation cheese. Stilton is one of the few cheeses granted a 'protected designation of origin' status by the European Commission, which in 1969 ruled that 'Stilton is blue or white cheese made from full cream milk, with no applied pressure, forming its own crust or coat and made in cylindrical form, the milk coming from English dairy herds in the district of Melton Mowbray and the surrounding areas falling within the counties of Leicestershire (now including Rutland), Derbyshire and Nottinghamshire'. There are strict codes for the quality of the cheese, and it can only be made in these designated counties. In Leicestershire, Melton Mowbray is recognised as one of the 'homes' of Stilton cheese, which is still made in the town today.

**MELTON MOWBRAY, THE MARKET
1932**   85169x

7

COCKL

RECIPE

STILTON AND CELERY SOUP

40g/1½ oz butter
1 onion, finely chopped
1 potato, cut into small cubes
1 whole head of celery, thinly sliced
900ml/1½ pints chicken or vegetable stock
115g/4oz Stilton cheese, crumbled
150ml/ ¼ pint single cream
Salt and freshly ground black pepper

Melt the butter in a large pan. Add the onion and cook over a medium heat for 5 minutes until it is transparent. Add the potato and celery and cook for a further 5 minutes until the vegetables begin to soften and brown. Add the stock, bring to the boil, then reduce heat, cover the pan and simmer for 30-40 minutes, until the vegetables are very soft.

Allow it to cool for a few minutes, then liquidize the soup in a blender, or pass it through a sieve, then return it to the pan and season to taste. Heat the soup through to just below the boil, then remove the pan from the heat, add the cheese and stir until it has melted.

Stir in the cream and reheat just before serving, being careful not to allow the soup to boil.

RECIPE

STILTON STUFFED PEARS

This makes an unusual snack or starter, using the Stilton cheese that is part of Leicestershire's food heritage. Stilton, pears and walnuts are a particularly fine combination of flavours.

> 2 large, ripe pears
> 115g/4oz Stilton cheese, firm but not hard
> 25g/1oz soft butter
> 1 tablespoonful double cream
> Freshly ground black pepper
> 25g/1oz walnuts, finely chopped, plus 4 walnut halves
> 4 crisp lettuce leaves
> 2 tablespoons lemon juice

Peel, halve and core the pears, hollowing them out carefully.

Cream together the cheese, butter, cream and black pepper, using either a blender or a bowl and wooden spoon. Add the chopped walnuts. Fill the centres of the pears with the mixture and stand each on a lettuce leaf on small plates. Put a half-walnut in the centre of each. Squeeze lemon juice over the unfilled parts of the pears to prevent them from discolouring, and serve as soon as possible after preparing.

Flavours of ...
LEICESTERSHIRE AND RUTLAND
CHEESE & VEGETABLE DISHES

RECIPE

POTTED STILTON

This is a good way of using up any leftover crumbs or pieces of Stilton cheese. It makes a tasty spread flavoured with mace and port wine, ideal for eating on toast, biscuits or oatcakes, and will keep well in the fridge for several weeks. This recipe makes enough for 4-6 servings, but if you only have a smaller amount of Stilton to use, reduce the proportions accordingly. This would make an unusual Christmas present for someone if packed in an attractive jar with a pretty label.

> 225g/8oz Stilton cheese
> 75g/3oz butter, softened to room temperature
> 2 teaspoonfuls port wine
> A pinch of ground mace
> Freshly ground black pepper
> A little melted butter (about 25g/1oz) to seal the top
>   of the mixture

Mash the Stilton cheese with a fork, then beat in the softened butter, ground mace, freshly ground black pepper and port wine until you have formed the mixture into a smooth cream. (Alternatively, the ingredients can all be mixed together in a blender or food processor.)

Pack the mixture into a small sterilised jar (or a number of smaller jars if preferred) and smooth off the surface, allowing space at the top for the butter seal. Melt the butter over a gentle heat, then pour a layer about 5mm (quarter inch) thick over the top of the mixture – if you pour it from the pan through the tines of a fork held at the rim, it will prevent the scum on the surface of the melted butter going on.

Cover the jars with their lids, and keep them in the fridge until

RECEIPE

LEICESTERSHIRE RAREBIT

As well as being renowned as a centre of Stilton cheese production, Leicestershire is also famous for its Red Leicester cheese, with a colour that ranges from russet to deep red. The cheese was originally coloured with carrot or beet juice, but nowadays annatto extract is used. It is made in flat 'cartwheels' and the best Red Leicester cheese has a grainy texture with a medium-strong flavour. It is an excellent cheese for cooking with as it melts well. Nowadays, the only manufacture of Red Leicester cheese actually based in the county is The Leicestershire Handmade Cheese Company run by the Clarke family from Sparkenhoe Farm at Upton, near Hinckley, in the south-west of the county.

Red Leicester cheese is used for this dish, known variously as Leicestershire Rarebit, Rabbit or Rare-bite. Traditionally, the rarebit was first made by soaking a toasted slice of bread in front of the open fire in red wine or beer. The thinly-cut cheese was then laid on top and left before the fire until the cheese was toasted and browned.

> 15g/ ½ oz butter
> 115g/4oz Red Leicester cheese
> 2 tablespoonfuls milk
> Salt and pepper
> 1 teaspoonful of made mustard
> Slices of hot buttered toast

Melt the butter in a saucepan and add the crumbled cheese.

Heat gently, stirring until melted, and gradually add the milk, doing this carefully to prevent the cheese becoming hard and lumpy.

Season with salt, pepper and mustard and pour over hot buttered toast.

RECIPE

STILTON AND BROCCOLI FLAN

This recipe makes a delicious savoury flan flavoured with Stilton cheese.

225g/8oz plain flour
115g/4oz butter or margarine
Salt and freshly ground black pepper
225g/8oz Stilton cheese, de-rinded and crumbled or cut
    into small pieces
2 large or 3 medium eggs
300ml/ ½ pint single cream
1 medium onion, peeled and finely chopped
1 tablespoonful olive or sunflower oil
250-275g/9-10oz trimmed weight of broccoli florets
1 tablespoonful chopped fresh chives
25g/1oz almond flakes, lightly toasted, to garnish

Pre-heat the oven to 200°C/400°F/Gas Mark 6, and place a baking tray in the oven to heat up. Grease a flan dish or tin 20-24cms (8-9 inches) square or diameter. Put the flour into a mixing bowl with a pinch of salt, and rub the butter or margarine into the flour until the mixture resembles fine breadcrumbs. Add 2-3 tablespoonfuls of cold water, just enough to mix it together to form a firm dough, then knead the dough lightly until it is smooth and elastic. Cover the dough with cling film and leave it in the fridge to 'rest' for 30 minutes. Roll out the pastry dough on a lightly floured surface, and use it to line the greased flan dish or tin. Place a piece of greaseproof paper with some baking beans on the pastry base, place the tin on the pre-heated baking tray in the oven (this helps the base to cook through) and bake blind for 10-15 minutes, until the pastry is set but not too browned. Remove from the oven and take out the greaseproof paper and baking beans. Reduce the heat of the oven to 190°C/375°F/Gas Mark 5 and put the baking tray back in the oven to heat up.

Cook the chopped onions in the oil in a pan until they are softened and translucent, then spread the onions on the cooked pastry base. Bring a pan of water to the boil, add the broccoli florets and bring the water back to the boil. As soon as the water is boiling again, remove the pan from the heat, drain the florets very well and leave them to steam off for a few minutes, then arrange them over the base of the pastry case. Spread the crumbled Stilton cheese over the florets. Whisk the eggs and cream together in a bowl, then mix in the chopped chives, freshly ground pepper and salt to taste. Take out the baking tray from the oven and stand the flan dish or tin on it. Pour the egg and cream mixture into the pastry case. Carefully return the tray to the oven with the flan dish or tin standing on it, and bake the flan at the reduced temperature for 40-45 minutes, until the filling is set and risen and firm to the touch. Sprinkle with the toasted almonds before serving.

This should not be eaten hot, straight from the oven, but leave it to cool a little and eat it warm or at room temperature, or otherwise eat it cold.

ROTHLEY, MILKING TIME c1955   R259001

RECIPE

LEICESTERSHIRE CHEESE AND HAM PUDDING

8 slices of bread, with the crusts removed
225g/8oz Red Leicester cheese, grated
175g/6oz ham or bacon, chopped into small pieces
25g/1oz butter or margarine
1 large onion
3 sticks of celery
300ml/ ½ pint milk
3 eggs
1 teaspoonful mustard powder
Salt and pepper

Pre-heat the oven to 180°C/350°F/Gas Mark 4.

Peel the onion, then chop the onion and celery into small pieces. Melt the butter in a frying pan and fry the onion and celery until soft and transparent. In a bowl, beat together the milk, eggs, mustard powder, salt and pepper. Dip the bread slices in the milk and egg mixture.

Reserve a small amount of the grated cheese, then place layers of onion and celery, grated cheese, chopped ham and slices of bread in a large, greased, shallow ovenproof dish, beginning and ending with slices of bread. Pour over any remaining milk mixture, and sprinkle the top with the reserved grated cheese.

Bake in the pre-heated oven for about 45 minutes, or until the top is golden brown.

THE BLABY SPECIAL TOMATO

Leicestershire is the home of a 'heritage' tomato, the 'Blaby Special'. This was a variety grown in the first half of the 20th century at a nursery and tomato farm in Blaby, a village a few miles south of Leicester. The Blaby Special tomato was specially developed for the local growing conditions and is notably red and juicy, and was very popular with local people. The tomato farm in Blaby went out of business in 1948 and it was thought that the Blaby Special tomato had gone for good, but a few years ago Dr Russell Sharp, a researcher from Lancaster Environment Centre at Lancaster University, managed to track down some seed in a seed bank in the Netherlands and grow it again. In 2006 he distributed Blaby Special tomato seed to local people in Blaby, and it is now being grown successfully on many local allotments. The reintroduction of the Blaby Special tomato to its home territory was celebrated in 2010 with the first Blaby Tomato Festival in the village.

KIBWORTH BEAUCHAMP, STATION STREET
c1955 K119017

ASHBY DE LA ZOUCH, MARKET STREET c1955 A212012

RECIPE

BRUSSELS SPROUTS WITH BACON

Leicestershire is one of England's main producers of Brussels sprouts.

675g/1½ lbs Brussels sprouts
6 rashers of streaky bacon
75g/3oz cheese of choice
25g/1oz fresh breadcrumbs

Wash and trim the Brussels sprouts, then cook them in boiling water until tender. Drain and put to one side. Chop the bacon into pieces and fry them for 10 minutes until they are cooked, then place the cooked bacon pieces in an ovenproof dish.

Toss the Brussels sprouts in the bacon fat left in the pan to coat them, then add them to the bacon in the dish. Grate the cheese and mix it with the breadcrumbs, and sprinkle the mixture on top of the sprouts and bacon.

Place the dish under a hot grill to brown the topping, and serve hot, either as a starter, a supper dish or as an accompaniment to meat as a main course.

THE UPPINGHAM TRENCHER

Uppingham is a charming town in Rutland with an attractive series of 17th and 18th-century buildings, and is also home to a famous public school. During the 18th century the town was known for trades such as building, stone quarrying, leather, metal and woodworking. Uppingham woodworkers were once well-known for their manufacture of trenchers – an old name for large, round wooden plates – and 'as round as an Uppingham trencher' was a popular saying.

UPPINGHAM, THE MARKET PLACE 1932 85156

RECIPES

BAKED STUFFED TROUT

Leicestershire's lakes and rivers are stocked with a wide variety of fish, including bream, carp, roach, tench and trout. Anglian Water's drinking water reservoir of Rutland Water near Oakham (one of the largest artificial lakes in Europe, and also the largest reservoir in England, by surface area) is also famous for the brown and rainbow trout that can be caught there. This is a traditional Leicestershire recipe for cooking trout.

> 4 trout, gutted and cleaned, with fins and gills removed
> 115g/4oz fresh breadcrumbs
> 115g/4oz butter
> Grated rind and juice of 1 lemon
> Salt and pepper to taste
> 1 egg yolk
> 25g/1oz plain flour
> 300ml/ ½ pint milk

Pre-heat the oven to 180°C/350°F/Gas Mark 4.

Melt half the butter in a heavy-bottomed pan, and add the breadcrumbs, lemon rind, salt and pepper. Remove from the heat and allow to cool a little, then beat in the egg yolk to form a firm stuffing. Use the stuffing to fill the cavity of each fish. Place the stuffed fish in a greased, ovenproof dish, dot the top with small knobs of butter, and bake in the pre-heated oven for 30 minutes.

Whilst the fish are cooking, melt the remaining butter in a saucepan, and stir in the flour to make a roux sauce. Cook gently for a few minutes, stirring occasionally, then gradually add the milk, stirring all time, and bring to the boil, still stirring continually, until the sauce has thickened. When the fish are cooked, pour the sauce into the dish with the fish and stir so that it combines with the fish juices. Add the lemon juice, then return the dish to the oven to cook for a further 5 minutes before serving.

20

LEICESTER FISH PIE

This dish differs from other more usual fish pie recipes where the fish is flaked in the sauce.

> 1kg/2 lbs potatoes, peeled and cut into chunks
> 750g/1½ lbs cod, hake or haddock fillets, skinned
>   and cut into 4 equal pieces
> Salt and pepper
> 900ml/1½ pints milk
> 75g/3oz butter
> 40g/1½ oz plain flour

Pre-heat the oven to 180°C/350°F/Gas Mark 4.

Boil the potatoes in salted water until tender (15-20 minutes). Grease a wide, shallow ovenproof dish and lay the pieces of fish in it, in two layers. Season with salt and pepper, and pour over 750ml/1¼ pints of the milk. Closely cover with foil and bake in the pre-heated oven for 25 minutes.

Drain the potatoes and mash with half the butter and 150ml (¼ pint) milk, beating until soft and creamy. Leave aside to cool, but do not chill in a fridge.

Just before removing the fish from the oven, melt 25g/1oz of the butter in a saucepan, sprinkle in the flour and cook, stirring all the time, for 1-2 minutes. Remove from the heat. Strain the cooking liquid from the fish, and gradually stir it into the butter and flour mixture (the roux). Return to the heat and cook, stirring, for 2-3 minutes, until thickened. Season to taste. Pour the sauce evenly over the fish, and leave to cool completely. When cooled, spread the mashed potato over the fish and lightly smooth over the surface, marking a decorative pattern on the top with a fork. Dot the surface with the remaining butter. Bake near the top of the pre-heated oven for about 25 minutes, until golden brown.

For special occasions, a luxury version of this pie can be made by stirring 85ml (3fl oz) of white wine into the roux before adding the milk, and 2 tablespoonfuls of double cream into the sauce just before pouring it over the fish.

ROBERT BAKEWELL (1725-1795)

A famous name in Britain's agricultural and food history was a Leicestershire man, the agricultural improver Robert Bakewell, who farmed at Dishley Grange near Loughborough. In the late 18th century Robert Bakewell elevated farming onto a whole new level that had not only national but world-wide importance. Until Bakewell's time, British cattle and sheep breeds were small and tough, and were not known for the quality of their meat. Robert Bakewell was a stockbreeder who set about improving the quality of his animals, pioneering first the Longhorn cattle breed, magnificent creatures whose rich milk was originally used to make Stilton cheese and whose meat is the true 'roast beef of Old England', and later the famous New Leicester sheep, which produced both good wool and good mutton and became the basis for many modern breeds and flocks. Robert Bakewell also created water meadows on his farm to enrich the grass. His neighbours thought he was mad but his experiments in both stockbreeding and agriculture proved him right, and his fame and influence grew. There were no agricultural colleges or other formal or scientific training for farmers at that time, so he was visited by a wide range of people, from students to royalty and aristocracy, all of whom were anxious to learn from him. However, although he was a gentle and amiable man he was also a staunch local Baptist, and he would never conduct business with anyone on a Sunday.

Robert Bakewell's heritage is, quite literally, alive and well to this day. The Blackbrook Herd of Longhorns bred by Pat and John Stanley at Grace Dieu, just off the A512 between Loughborough and Ashby de la Zouch, is world famous and the genes of these cattle have been exported all over the globe. The herd has won countless awards and prizes. The beef produced from these animals is of the most superb quality. Like many another of Loughborough's sons and daughters, Robert Bakewell's fame, reputation and heritage are better known outside his native town than within it.

RECIPE

BEEF STEAKS WITH CREAMY STILTON SAUCE

This easy recipe uses Stilton cheese to make a rich creamy sauce to accompany good quality British beef steaks. Do not add salt to the sauce - there is already enough salt in the cheese to season it. This amount serves 4 people – reduce the amounts for less.

> 4 good quality sirloin or fillet steaks, each trimmed
>   weight of about 110-175g (4-6 oz)
> Freshly ground black pepper
> 200ml/7 fl oz stock
> 300ml/10 fl oz double cream
> 175g/6oz Stilton cheese, crumbled

To make the sauce, heat the stock in a saucepan until it comes to the boil. Add the crumbled Stilton cheese and stir until the cheese has melted. Add the cream and a twist of freshly ground black pepper, bring back to the boil, then allow to boil and bubble for about 5 minutes, until the sauce has reduced down and thickened slightly, stirring regularly to make sure it does not stick and burn. When the sauce is ready, reduce the heat to very low and keep warm, stirring occasionally, whilst you cook the steaks.

Place the trimmed steaks on a grill rack, or on a griddle or frying pan that has been preheated over a high heat until hot, but not smoking. (If the pan is too hot, the outside of the steak will burn before the inside is done, if it is too cold, your steaks will be tough.) Brush the steaks with a little oil and season to taste with a little freshly ground black pepper. Cook the steaks for 2 – 5 minutes on each side, according to the thickness of the meat and how well done you like your steaks (see below), then leave to rest', to let the meat 'relax' and tenderise after cooking – remove the steaks from the grill rack or pan, cover them with foil and leave in a warm place for a few minutes, until the sauce is ready.

> Suggested cooking and resting times for steaks:
> Rare: 1-2 minutes per side – rest for 6-8 minutes
> Medium rare: 2-3 minutes per side – rest for 5 minutes
> Medium: 3-4 minutes per side – rest for 4 minutes
> Well done: 4-6 minutes per side – rest for 1 minute

LOUGHBOROUGH, THE CATTLE MARKET c1950 LI97015

MELTON MOWBRAY PORK PIES

Melton Mowbray in north Leicestershire is a historic market town that is renowned the world over for its famous pork pie. It is no coincidence that Melton Mowbray's two most renowned delicacies – Stilton cheese and pork pies – originated in the same region. Pigs thrive on whey, which is the chief by-product of the cheese-making for which this region is famous, and so Stilton cheese and pork pies were made side by side in the area.

The Melton Mowbray Pork Pie originated in Melton in 1831, linked with Leicestershire's strong foxhunting tradition. Many years ago Leicestershire became a centre for foxhunting, especially around Quorn, Belvoir, Melton Mowbray and Market Harborough, and farmers created special woodlands as cover for foxes that are still part of the landscape today. Melton Mowbray was situated within easy reach of all the premier Shire foxhunting packs and Edward Adcock, who ran a bakery adjacent to the Fox Inn in Leicester Street, recognised the popularity of his cold meat pies among the visiting foxhunting fraternity – the pies were a favourite dish served at high teas after a long day's hunting. Adcock decided to market his pies in London, which proved to be a huge success. By 1840 the increased demand allowed Enoch Evans to set up a rival business in the Beast Market (now Sherrard Street), and the popularity of the Melton Mowbray pork pie began to grow. These hand-raised pies are uniquely rounded with a distinctive bulbous shape, and are flavoured with sage and a hint of anchovy essence. They are made from the finest British lean, fresh (uncured) pork, coarsely chopped, encased in rich and crunchy pastry. This use of fresh, rather than cured, meat gives the filling of the Melton Mowbray pork pie its characteristic grey colour, rather than the pink of other pork pies, which use cured pork. Dickinson & Morris, who run Ye Olde Pork Pie Shoppe in Nottingham Street (seen on the left of photograph M60075, opposite) are the last remaining firm in Melton to bake the authentic pies on their shop premises. The bakery was founded in 1851 and has since become a huge tourist attraction, with as many as 250,000 visitors each year.

MELTON MOWBRAY, SHERRARD STREET c1955 M60036

MELTON MOWBRAY, NOTTINGHAM STREET c1955 M60075

RECIPE

QUORN BACON ROLL

This savoury suet pudding filled with bacon, onions and herbs is named after the Leicestershire village of Quorn and was made by thrifty local housewives in the past as an economical way of feeding large, hungry families. The tradition of making this dish in Quorn is kept alive by the Quorn Bacon Roll Day, when local cooks compete to make the best Bacon Roll.

For the pastry
175g/6oz self-raising flour
115g/4oz shredded suet
Salt and freshly ground black
  pepper
About 6 tablespoonfuls of water
2 heaped tablespoonfuls of
  chopped fresh parsley

For the filling
225g/8oz unsmoked back
  bacon rashers, left whole
225g/8oz cooked ham
  trimmings or unsmoked bacon
  bits, chopped into pieces

1 large onion, peeled and sliced
25g/1oz butter
Half a teaspoonful soft brown
  sugar
1 dessertspoonful of chopped
  fresh sage (or a teaspoonful of
  chopped dried sage)
A small amount of stock
1 tablespoonful sunflower oil
  (or dripping, if you have it)
Salt and freshly ground black
  pepper

Melt the butter in a pan, add the onions and sprinkle the brown sugar over them, to help the onions caramelise. Fry the onions over a gentle heat until they are soft and lightly browned, stirring occasionally so they don't stick and burn. Remove the cooked onions from the pan and put to one side. Heat the oil (or the dripping, if using) in the same pan and fry the bacon rashers until they are cooked through, then add the cooked onions to the pan, together with the chopped ham or bacon bits and the sage, and season to taste with a little salt, if needed, and freshly ground black pepper. Mix together, then turn out the mixture onto a plate and leave to cool whilst you make the suet pastry.

Sieve the flour into a bowl, then season to taste with salt and pepper and stir in the chopped fresh parsley and the suet. Mix together to a dough, adding just enough cold water to form a soft dough which is still firm enough to roll out – don't make it too wet and sticky. Knead the dough for a few minutes and form it into a ball, then roll it out on a floured surface into a rectangle about 1cm (½ inch) thick. Lay the bacon rashers across the length of the pastry, leaving 1cm (½ inch) around the edges, then cover with the rest of the mixture, and sprinkle over a small amount of stock, to keep the mixture moist. Roll it all up loosely like a Swiss roll to make a roll about 18cm (7 inches) wide. Dampen the ends and pinch the edges firmly together to seal them. Loosely wrap the roll in a piece of buttered, pleated greaseproof paper and then in a further piece of buttered, pleated foil (to allow room for expansion during cooking), pleating the open edges tightly together to seal them well. Seal the ends of the wrapping and tie them with string, again leaving enough room for the Bacon Roll to swell during cooking.

Fill the bottom half of a steamer or fish kettle with water and bring it to the boil. Put the Bacon Roll in the top of the steamer or fish kettle, cover with the lid and steam it over the boiling water for about 2½ hours, topping up the pan with more boiling water if necessary, to ensure it does not boil dry. If you haven't got a steamer or fish kettle, lower the Bacon Roll into a large saucepan of boiling water, cover the pan with its lid and boil for 2½ hours, topping up the pan with boiling water as necessary so it doesn't boil dry.

When cooked, lift out the Bacon Roll, unwrap and place on an ovenproof serving dish in a pre-heated oven for 5 minutes to finish, at 180°C/350°F/Gas Mark 4. Serve cut into slices, with potatoes and root vegetables like turnips, carrots, parsnips or swede.

RECIPE

LEICESTERSHIRE MEDLEY PIE

The use of both meat and fruit in Leicestershire Medley Pie, together with the flavouring of ginger, suggests that this is a very old traditional recipe, probably dating back to medieval times. A 'medley pie' is a savoury pie made with a combination of ingredients, and this is an excellent way of using up various cuts of left-over cooked meats, whatever is available.

Use a combination of cold fat bacon with an equal quantity of leftover roast pork, beef or lamb, cut into thick slices. Cut 2 or 3 cooking apples into quarters, but do not peel them. Remove the cores, and cut the apples into slices. Arrange the meat and apple slices in alternate layers in a pie dish, seasoning the layers as you go with salt, pepper and a little ground ginger to taste.

Pour in about 300ml (half a pint) of beer or ale, just enough to cover the filling.

Grease the rim of the pie dish, and cover the filling with shortcrust pastry made with lard or dripping from the roast joint as the fat if possible, sealing the edges well.

Brush the pastry with beaten egg and bake the pie in a moderate oven (180°C/350°F/Gas Mark 4) for about one hour, or until the pastry is crisp and golden.

LUTTERWORTH, CHURCH STREET
AND THE CHURCH c1955 L307002

COACH
&
HORSES

RECIPE

TOAD IN THE HOLE WITH RUTLAND SAUSAGES

Rutland is famous for its meaty and highly seasoned Rutland Sausages, but there are several varieties of these. Dickinson & Morris in Melton Mowbray sell a version made with Stilton Cheese, mustard seeds and herbs, and Grassmere Farm at Deeping St James in Lincolnshire produce a variety flavoured with garlic that was originally created for the Ram Jam Inn at Stretton near Oakham, whilst Nelsons the butchers, with shops in Oakham and Uppingham, advertise their Rutland Sausages, made with 80% pork and flavoured with a secret blend of seasonings, as 'the original recipe'. They are all great sausages – use your own favourite variety of Rutland Sausages for this recipe!

> 450g/1 lb Rutland Sausages
> 175g/6oz plain flour
> A pinch of salt
> 2 eggs
> 600ml/1 pint milk and water mixed
> 15g/ ½ oz lard or dripping

Make the batter 1 hour before you start cooking the dish. Put the flour in a bowl with the salt, make a well in the centre and break in the eggs. Beat them into the flour, gradually adding the milk and water to make a smooth, creamy batter. Beat it well, then leave to stand for 1 hour. (This can also be prepared in a liquidizer if preferred.)

Pre-heat the oven to 220°C/425°F/Gas Mark 7. Melt the lard or dripping in a frying pan and brown the sausages nicely all over (this gives a better flavour than cooking the sausages in the oven). Pour the fat and sausages into a 30cm (12 inch) roasting tin. Place the tin in the oven for a few minutes to heat through, then remove from the oven, pour in the prepared batter and replace the tin in the oven. When the batter is nicely puffed up, reduce the oven temperature to 190°C/375°F/Gas Mark 5, and continue cooking until well-risen and golden brown – the total cooking time from start to finish should be 35-40 minutes.

THE RUTLAND DWARF

Rutland's county motto means 'much in little', which is very apt for the smallest county in England, which in 1997 was restored as a county in its own right after unpopular local government reorganisation of 1974 merged it with Lincolnshire. Oakham, the county town of Rutland, was the birthplace in 1619 of Sir Jeffrey Hudson (1619-1682), 'the shortest knight in the kingdom'. Known as 'The Rutland Dwarf', he was only 18 inches tall from the ages of eight to thirty. Later he grew to 3 feet 6 inches. When he was nine he was taken up to the Duke of Buckingham's mansion at Burley-on-the-Hill on the occasion of the visit of Charles I and his queen, Henrietta Maria, and as a dinner-time diversion he jumped out of a cold pie dressed in a tiny suit of armour. So impressed was the queen that she took Jeffrey into her service and had him knighted. He became a darling of the court, was made a captain of horse and had many adventures in his life, including being taken prisoner by pirates and nearly drowning in a wash basin!

OAKHAM, HIGH STREET 1927 80284

RECIPE

MARKET HARBOROUGH PORK AND APPLE PIE

This recipe is a version of the 'fidget', or 'fitchett', pies that are also found in other parts of the country. In her book 'Food in England' (1954), Dorothy Hartley noted that particularly good versions of these pies were made around Market Harborough.

<u>For the filling:</u>
675g/1½ lbs fresh pork, trimmed of fat and cut into cubes
25g/1oz plain flour, seasoned with a little salt and pepper
1 tablespoonful oil
2 onions, peeled and roughly chopped into pieces
2 sticks of celery, chopped into small pieces
450ml/ ¾ pint stock
1 tablespoonful Worcestershire Sauce
3 large cooking apples
Salt and pepper to taste

<u>For the pastry</u>
225g/8oz plain flour
115g/4oz butter or margarine
A pinch of salt
A little water to mix
A little milk or beaten egg to glaze

Toss the cubes of pork in the seasoned flour so that all the sides are coated. Heat some of the oil in a large saucepan, and fry the cubes of meat in batches for a few minutes, until they are lightly browned on all sides, adding more of the oil as necessary. Remove the meat from the pan. Fry the prepared onions and celery in the remaining oil until soft. Add the stock and Worcestershire Sauce, and season to taste with a little salt and pepper. Return the meat to the pan, bring to the boil then reduce the heat to low, cover the pan with its lid and simmer gently for 30 minutes. The flour on the meat will thicken the gravy but will also cause the mixture to stick to the bottom of the pan, so stir the mixture thoroughly from time to time to prevent sticking and burning. Whilst the meat is cooking, make the pastry. Put the flour into a mixing bowl and add a pinch of salt. Rub the fat into the flour until the mixture resembles breadcrumbs. Mix in enough cold water to form a soft dough and knead lightly, then wrap the pastry dough in cling film or place it in a plastic bag and leave it to 'rest' in the fridge until ready to use.

When the pork mixture is ready to use, pre-heat the oven to 200°C/400°F/Gas Mark 6 and grease the rim of a large pie dish. Peel and core the cooking apples and cut them into slices. Place a layer of apple slices on the bottom of the dish. Pour the pork mixture on top of the apples, then top the mixture with the remaining apple slices. Roll out the pastry on a lightly floured surface and place it over the ingredients in the pie dish to make a lid, moistening the edges to seal them to the rim of the dish and pressing round firmly. Use a sharp knife to cut a cross in the middle of the pastry lid to let out the steam during cooking, then brush the pastry lid with a little milk or beaten egg to glaze. Bake in the pre-heated oven for 25-30 minutes, until the pastry is crisp and golden.

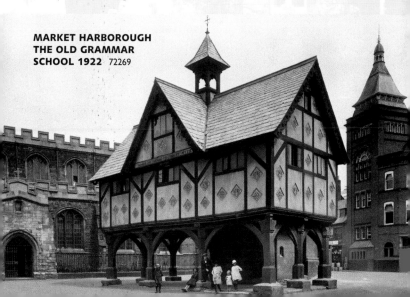

MARKET HARBOROUGH
THE OLD GRAMMAR
SCHOOL 1922 72269

HALLATON HARE PIE SCRAMBLING AND BOTTLE KICKING'

The tradition of 'Hallaton Hare Pie Scrambling and Bottle Kicking' takes place each year on Easter Monday just outside Market Harborough, between the villages of Hallaton and Medbourne, and dates back 1,000 years to medieval times. The aim of the annual event is to wrestle a small keg of ale back to your parish. Part of the tradition involves a large hare pie being specially baked for the occasion, pieces of which are thrown into the crowds at Hare Pie Bank for people to 'scramble' for. There is then a bottle-kicking contest, when teams from the villages of Hallaton and Medbourne try to be the first to kick their own bottle down the hill and across the brook. The boisterous event dates back to medieval times, when a piece of land was left to the local rector on the condition that he provided hare pies, ale and loaves 'to be scrambled for' by local people on each succeeding Easter Monday at the place called Hare Pie Bank. It is one of Britain's oldest and most eccentric traditional events, and the wild free-for-all attracts large crowds of spectators every year.

JOHNNY COLE

This epitaph was recorded on a now-disappeared grave in Melton Mowbray:

Here lies Johnny Cole,
Who died, upon my soul,
After eating a plentiful dinner;
While chewing his crust,
He was turned into dust,
With his crimes undigested – poor sinner.

FOXTON, THE GRAND UNION CANAL
c1960 F159004

LEICESTER, GRANBY STREET 1949 L144032

The city of Leicester is famous for its Victorian architecture. Some of the superb buildings of this period are the HSBC Bank in the city centre (on the corner of Granby Street and Bishop Street), the former Singer Building in the High Street (now nos 76-88 Coronation Building) and the 'Turkey Café' (in Granby Street, between Halford Street and Rutland Street, and opposite Bishop Street),which features a number of portrayals of turkeys, on either side of the entrance and in an attractive mosaic on the top floor, a play on the Turkish-themed design of the building. The architect was Arthur Wakerley, a Melton Mowbray man who later became Mayor of Leicester, who also designed the Singer Building. Leicester is now moving forward into the 21st century as a vibrant modern city with a diverse ethnic population. Life in Leicester has been greatly enriched by the various festivals and cultures of its citizens, such as the Diwali lights and the Caribbean Carnival, and their food and restaurants. Fruit, vegetables and spices from all over the world can be found at Leicester Market, the largest covered market in Europe. Modern Leicester is particularly famous for its renowned Asian restaurants, many of which are to be found along Belgrave Road, an area known as the 'Golden Mile', making Leicester the 'Curry Capital' of the UK.

LEICESTER, MARKET STREET 1949 LI44016

**LEICESTER
THE CLOCK TOWER
AND BELGRAVE GATE
1949** L144010

RECIPES

LEICESTER PUDDING

This recipe for a steamed sponge pudding cooked in a generous coating of jam comes from a 1930s' cookbook. Good old-fashioned comfort food for a cold winter's day!

> 225g/8oz self-raising flour
> 115g/4oz butter or margarine
> 115g/4oz caster sugar
> 2 eggs, beaten
> 225g/8oz jam of choice – raspberry jam is
> particularly good
> A pinch of salt
> A little milk

In a large mixing bowl, cream together the butter or margarine and the sugar until pale and fluffy. Gradually add the beaten eggs into the mixture, beating thoroughly until combined, adding a small amount of the flour if necessary to prevent the mixture curdling. Add the rest of the flour and a pinch of salt and mix well, adding a little milk – just enough to form the mixture into a smooth batter.

Butter the inside of a large pudding basin, and line the inside and bottom of the basin with a liberal coating of jam. Pour in the batter. Cover the pudding basin with its lid if you have one, or with a covering made of pleated greaseproof paper (to allow room for expansion during cooking), buttered on the inside, and then cover that with a pleated piece of foil, and tie down securely with string.

Place the pudding bowl in a very large saucepan with a lid, standing on a trivet or an inverted saucer in the pan. Fill the pan up to halfway up the pudding basin with boiling water, cover the pan with its lid then place on the heat and bring the water back to the boil. Steam the pudding for 2-2½ hours, making sure that the pan does not boil dry, and topping it up with more boiling water if necessary. When cooked, turn out the pudding onto a serving dish and serve with custard or cream.

LEICESTERSHIRE PUDDING

This hearty suet pudding stuffed with dried fruit and spices is another traditional dish linked with Leicestershire's foxhunting heritage, and is also known as Hunting Pudding – it was often served hot at dinner after a day spent hunting, or could be eaten cold, cut into slices and carried in saddlebags, for riders to eat as a snack whilst they were out following the hounds. The recipe dates back to the 18th century, when it would have been boiled in a pudding cloth, resulting in a ball-shaped pudding; it was recorded as 'Hunting Pudding' in a recipe book of 1764 called 'English Housewifry' with the note that 'you must have a little white wine and butter for your sauce' to accompany it – nowadays, try serving it with whipped cream or custard made with the addition of a teaspoonful of brandy.

225g/8oz seedless raisins
50g/2oz currants
115g/4oz self-raising flour
115g/4oz shredded suet
115g/4oz soft dark brown sugar
Half a teaspoonful ground nutmeg
Half a teaspoonful ground cinnamon
The finely grated zest of 1 lemon
2 eggs, beaten
1 tablespoonful brandy (optional, but it improves the flavour)
A little milk, for mixing

In a large bowl, mix together the dried fruit, flour, suet and sugar. Add the nutmeg, cinnamon and lemon zest, then beat in the eggs and the brandy, if using. Combine it all together well, adding a little milk if necessary to make a stiff mixture.

Butter the inside of a large pudding basin. Pour the mixture into the pudding basin and smooth the top. Cover the basin with a double layer of buttered greaseproof paper with a folded pleat in the middle, to allow room for expansion during the cooking process. Cover this with a piece of foil, also pleated in the middle, and tie it all down firmly with string. If you have a steamer, place the basin in a steamer basket over boiling water; otherwise stand the basin on a trivet or an upturned saucer in a large saucepan and fill the pan with boiling water to come halfway up the basin. Cover the steamer or pan with its lid, bring the water to the boil and steam the pudding for 2 hours. Top up the pan with more boiling water from time to time, and do not allow the pan to boil dry. When cooked, remove the pudding from the pan and turn it out onto a serving dish. Serve hot, cut into slices, with custard or cream. Any leftover pudding can be eaten cold as a cake.

BELVOIR CASTLE

It was at Belvoir Castle in Rutland that the ritual of afternoon teatime originated. Anna Maria Stanhope, the 7th Duchess of Bedford, was visiting Belvoir in the 1840s and found herself in need of extra sustenance to see her through the period from luncheon until the formal dinner in the evening. She asked the servants to bring tea-making equipment and some bread and butter discreetly to her room, and found this extra snack so enjoyable that she invited her friends to join her in the late afternoons to partake of a cup of tea with a dainty sandwich or a small cake. Fanny Kemble, a famous actress of the time, visited the Duchess at Belvoir Castle in 1842, and later wrote: 'My first introduction to "afternoon tea" took place during this visit to Belvoir, when I received on several occasions private and rather mysterious invitations to the Duchess of Bedford's room, and found her with a "small and select" circle of female guests of the castle, busily employed in brewing and drinking tea, with her grace's own private tea-kettle. I do not believe that now universally honoured and observed institution of "five-o'clock-tea" dates farther back in the annals of English civilisation that this very private and, I think, rather shamefaced practice of it.' The Duchess continued the custom when she returned to London, and soon every fashionable hostess was following her lead.

BELVOIR CASTLE c1965 B63190

RECITE

BELVOIR CASTLE BUNS

The recipe for these buns goes back to the 1860s, when they were made at Belvoir Castle and were said to be a particular favourite of the seventh Duke of Rutland (1818-1906).

> 450g/1 lb plain flour
> 115g/4oz currants
> 115g/4oz sugar
> 150ml/ ¼ pint milk
> 50g/2oz butter
> ½ oz fresh yeast or ¼ oz dried yeast
> 1 teaspoonful salt
> A little milk to finish

Place the flour in a mixing bowl, and stir in the salt. Add the butter and rub it into the flour until the mixture resembles fine breadcrumbs, then mix in the sugar. Warm the milk until it is lukewarm, add the yeast and 1 teaspoonful of sugar, and stir until dissolved. Leave the yeast mixture to stand, covered, in a warm place until it is frothy. When it is ready, pour the mixture into the flour and mix well, then add half the currants.

Knead the dough on a lightly floured surface for about 10 minutes, until it is smooth and pliable. Place the dough in a bowl, cover with a cloth and leave it in a warm place to rise, until it has doubled in size, then knock back the dough and knead it again. Roll out the dough to make a square about 1cm (half an inch) thick. Sprinkle the dough with the remaining currants, then roll it up like a Swiss roll. Cut the dough into slices about 2.5cm (1 inch) wide, and place them on a greased baking sheet, cut side up, then leave the baking sheet in a warm place for about 30 minutes, for the buns to rise.

When ready to bake, brush the buns with a little milk to glaze them, and bake in a pre-heated oven (220°C/425°F/Gas Mark 7) for 10-12 minutes.

MELTON HUNT CAKE

Since 1954, Dickinson & Morris in Melton Mowbray has been the exclusive producer of the Melton Hunt Cake, as well as its famous Melton Mowbray pork pies. This cake is made using a mixture of dried fruit, with a generous helping of old Jamaica rum. Like the Melton Mowbray pork pies, Hunt Cake was greatly enjoyed by the visiting hunting community in the past – the riders would enjoy a slice with a glass of sherry on horseback at the meet whilst waiting for the hunt to begin.

MELTON MOWBRAY, THE BELVOIR HUNT c1955 M60056

RECIPE

LEICESTER SAND CAKE

The use of cornflour in this delicious and unusual cake produces a light and smooth texture.

For the cake:
75g/3oz butter or margarine
115g/4oz caster sugar
2 eggs, beaten
Finely grated rind of 1 lemon
115g/4oz cornflour
25g/1oz plain flour
1½ teaspoonfuls baking powder

For the icing:
3 teaspoonfuls lemon juice
1 teaspoonful water
115g/4oz sifted icing sugar

Pre-heat the oven to 180°C/350°F/Gas Mark 4 and grease a 450g (1 lb) loaf tin.

Cream the butter or margarine with the sugar until light, fluffy and pale. Gradually beat in the eggs and add the lemon rind. Sift the cornflour with the flour and baking powder, and fold into the mixture. Turn into the greased loaf tin. Bake in the pre-heated oven for about 50 minutes, or until a skewer inserted into the cake comes out clean. Turn out onto a wire rack and cool.

To make the icing, mix the lemon juice and water into the icing sugar in a small saucepan. Stir over a low heat until melted and just warm, and immediately pour over the cake and allow the icing to run down the sides. Leave to set, and serve in slices.

ANYONE FOR CHEESECAKES?

Leicestershire has a place in food history linked with the popular delicacy of cheesecake. Although the earliest English cheesecake recipe occurs in a 14th-century recipe collection called 'The Forme of Cury', the first recorded mention of actually using 'cheese for tarts' comes from the accounts for the year 1265 of Eleanor, Countess of Leicester, the wife of Simon de Montfort, 6th Earl of Leicester who led the baronial revolt against Henry III. He is one of the four famous people in Leicester's history commemorated with a statue on the 19th-century Gothic-style Clock Tower in the city (see photograph L144010 on page 41).

However, the traditional 'cheesecakes' of Leicestershire are not the creamy desserts on a biscuit base that most people think of as cheesecakes today, but small cakes baked in a pastry case with a filling made of curd cheese and dried fruit. In some parts of the county it was the custom in the past to make them to be eaten at Whitsun in May.

In recent years the 'cheesecakes' of this type sold in Leicestershire, such as those made by Wesses Bakery in Market Harborough, have had to be renamed as 'curd cakes' to comply with Food Labelling Regulations, so as not to confuse customers used to modern-style cheesecakes. However, 'cheesecakes' is the traditional name they were known by, so that is what the recipe on the opposite page is called! These cakes are traditionally made with curd cheese, which is similar to cream cheese but with a lower fat content. This gives the best flavour to the filling, but if curd cheese proves hard to find, you can use cottage cheese instead, drained of its liquid and then either sieved or zapped with a blender until it is smooth, or a low fat cream cheese or soft cheese like Philadelphia. Another alternative you can use is ricotta cheese.

RECIPE

LEICESTERSHIRE CHEESECAKES

350g/12oz shortcrust pastry, made with butter for the fat and
    with the addition of a dessertspoonful of icing sugar for
    best results

50g/2oz butter

50g/2oz caster sugar

1 egg

115g/4oz curd cheese, or alternative (see note on opposite
    page)

50g/2oz cake crumbs

50g/2oz currants

1 tablespoonful of single cream

A little freshly grated nutmeg

Grated rind of 1 lemon

1 tablespoonful of brandy – don't leave this out unless you
    have to, it makes all the difference to the flavour of the filling

Pre-heat the oven to 180°C/350°F/Gas Mark 4. Grease 12 deep
patty tins. Roll out the pastry quite thin on a lightly floured surface
and use it to line the patty tins. Prick the pastry cases with a fork to
remove any air bubbles under the pastry and make holes for air to
escape whilst cooking.

Cream the butter and sugar together until light and fluffy, then
beat in the egg and the cheese. Mix in the cake crumbs, the
currants and the cream, then add the lemon rind, brandy and a
little freshly grated nutmeg, to taste. Beat the mixture well to mix
it all together. Spoon the mixture into the pastry cases, but only up
to about three-quarters full. Bake in the pre-heated oven for 25-30
minutes, until the filling is risen and firm to the touch.

These can be eaten hot with custard or cream as a pudding course,
or cold as cakes.

RECIPE

BOSWORTH JUMBLES

These small 'S'-shaped cakes were said to have been a speciality of King Richard III's cook in the 15th century. King Richard III was killed at the Battle of Bosworth, near Market Bosworth in Leicestershire, in 1485 when his forces were defeated by the army of Henry Tudor, who then became Henry VII. There is a tradition that the recipe for Bosworth Jumbles was found dropped on the battlefield! In former times jumbles were made in the form of two interlaced rings, and their name derives from the word 'gemmel' for a twin finger ring.

225g/8oz self-raising flour
175g/6oz butter or margarine
175g/6oz caster sugar
1 egg
1 teaspoonful grated lemon rind
Half a teaspoonful almond essence (optional)
Icing sugar to dredge

Pre-heat the oven to 180°C/350°F/Gas Mark 4.

Cream the butter or margarine with the sugar until it is light and fluffy. Carefully beat in the egg, a little at a time, and the lemon rind and almond essence, if used. Gradually mix in the sieved flour, and mix it all to a stiff consistency. Take small pieces of the dough, roll them lightly in your hands into a sausage shape, then bend each piece into an 'S' shape. Place the jumbles on greased and floured baking sheets, well spaced out so that they will not run together while baking. Bake in the pre-heated oven for about 10-15 minutes, giving them a quarter turn after 5-7 minutes so that they all bake evenly. Transfer the cooked jumbles to a wire rack and leave them to cool completely, then dredge with icing sugar before serving.

MARKET BOSWORTH, MARKET PLACE c1955 M233012

THATCH GROBY POOL WITH PANCAKES

A local saying from Leicestershire linked with food derives from Groby Pool, four miles north-west of Leicester. Once it was larger, but its 40 acres qualified the pool as the largest sheet of water in the county until the 19th century, hence the Leicestershire saying 'to thatch Groby Pool with pancakes', which indicates any impossible undertaking.

RECIPES

RED LEICESTER CHEESE SCONES

This recipe is for tasty savoury scones flavoured with Red Leicester cheese. These are very good eaten just on their own, or split and spread with butter, or can be served with pieces of cheese. They are also nice to take on picnics and also make a great accompaniment to a bowl of hearty country-style soup, such as leek and potato. You could also make very small scones and serve them as party nibbles, spread with a herby cream cheese. This amount makes 6-8 rustic-style scones.

> 225g/8oz self raising flour
> ½ teaspoonful baking powder
> 1 teaspoonful English mustard powder
> ½ teaspoonful salt
> Pinch of pepper
> 50g/2oz butter or margarine, cut into small pieces
> 115g/4oz Red Leicester cheese, grated
> 1 large egg, beaten
> 2-3 tablespoonfuls milk

Pre-heat the oven to 220°C/425°F/Gas Mark 7 and grease a baking tray.

Sift together the flour, baking powder, mustard powder and salt and pepper into a mixing bowl. Use your fingers to rub in the butter or margarine, then mix in the grated cheese.

Mix together the beaten egg and the milk, then pour it into the bowl and use a round-bladed knife to cut the liquid into the flour mixture. Bring it all together with your hands to form a firm dough – make sure that it is well mixed but be careful not to overwork it.

Place the dough on a lightly floured surface and gently press it out to be about 1cm (½ inch) thick. Use a sharp knife to cut the dough into rectangular shapes, about 8cms (3 inches) square. Place the pieces on the baking tray and bake in the pre-heated oven for 12-15 minutes, until they are risen and just golden. Place on a wire rack and leave to cool. These are best eaten on the same day as they are made.

LEICESTERSHIRE APPLE SHORTCAKE

This recipe for a delicious shortcake with an apple layer in the middle was found in a cookbook from the 1930s. It can be eaten either as a cold slice at teatime, or hot from the oven with cream or custard for a pudding course.

> 225g/8oz self-raising flour
> 150g/5oz butter, softened to room temperature
> 115g/4oz caster sugar
> 1 extra dessertspoonful of caster sugar
> 1 large egg, beaten
> 450g/1 lb cooking apples
> A pinch of salt

Pre-heat the oven to 180°C/350°F/Gas Mark 4. Peel and core the apples and chop them into pieces. Cook them over a gentle heat with 1 tablespoonful of water and one dessertspoonful of sugar until they are soft and fluffy. Put the cooked apple puree into a sieve or colander and allow the liquid to strain off, to leave a thick apple purée. Leave to cool whilst you prepare the shortcake mixture. Cream the softened butter and sugar together in a bowl, then add the beaten egg, a little at a time, and beat well, adding a little of the flour to prevent the mixture curdling. Add in the rest of the flour and a pinch of salt and mix together well – the mixture will be very stiff, but do not be tempted to add milk to make it easier to work. Alternatively, the ingredients can all be mixed together in a food mixer or processor if preferred.

Grease a shallow baking tin, about 18-20cms (7-8 inches) square or round. Press half the dough into the tin. Spread the apple purée in a layer over the dough in the tin, then cover with the remaining dough. This might be easier to do if you roll out the dough on a well-floured surface and carefully roll up over the rolling pin to put over the apple (the dough will be sticky!). Otherwise, flatten out pieces of the dough and 'patchwork' it over the apple to cover it. Don't worry if it looks a bit untidy or you leave a few small gaps, it will be fine when the cake has cooked. Bake in the pre-heated oven for about 40- 45 minutes, until the sponge has risen and is cooked and golden brown. Take out of the oven and if not eating hot as a pudding course, leave it to cool completely in the tin before cutting it into squares or slices. Store in an airtight container.

FRANCIS FRITH

PIONEER VICTORIAN PHOTOGRAPHER

Francis Frith, founder of the world-famous photographic archive, was a complex and multi-talented man. A devout Quaker and a highly successful Victorian businessman, he was philosophical by nature and pioneering in outlook. By 1855 he had already established a wholesale grocery business in Liverpool, and sold it for the astonishing sum of £200,000, which is the equivalent today of over £15,000,000. Now in his thirties, and captivated by the new science of photography, Frith set out on a series of pioneering journeys up the Nile and to the Near East.

INTRIGUE AND EXPLORATION

He was the first photographer to venture beyond the sixth cataract of the Nile. Africa was still the mysterious 'Dark Continent', and Stanley and Livingstone's historic meeting was a decade into the future. The conditions for picture taking confound belief. He laboured for hours in his wicker dark-room in the sweltering heat of the desert, while the volatile chemicals fizzed dangerously in their trays. Back in London he exhibited his photographs and was 'rapturously cheered' by members of the Royal Society. His reputation as a photographer was made overnight.

VENTURE OF A LIFE-TIME

By the 1870s the railways had threaded their way across the country, and Bank Holidays and half-day Saturdays had been made obligatory by Act of Parliament. All of a sudden the working man and his family were able to enjoy days out, take holidays, and see a little more of the world.

With typical business acumen, Francis Frith foresaw that these new tourists would enjoy having souvenirs to commemorate their days out. For the next thirty years he travelled the country by train and by pony and trap, producing fine photographs of seaside resorts and beauty spots that were keenly bought by millions of Victorians. These prints were painstakingly pasted into family albums and pored over during the dark nights of winter, rekindling precious memories of summer excursions. Frith's studio was soon supplying retail shops all over the country, and by 1890 F Frith & Co had become the greatest specialist photographic publishing company in the world, with over 2,000 sales outlets, and pioneered the picture postcard.

FRANCIS FRITH'S LEGACY

Francis Frith had died in 1898 at his villa in Cannes, his great project still growing. By 1970 the archive he created contained over a third of a million pictures showing 7,000 British towns and villages.

Frith's legacy to us today is of immense significance and value, for the magnificent archive of evocative photographs he created provides a unique record of change in the cities, towns and villages throughout Britain over a century and more. Frith and his fellow studio photographers revisited locations many times down the years to update their views, compiling for us an enthralling and colourful pageant of British life and character.

We are fortunate that Frith was dedicated to recording the minutiae of everyday life. For it is this sheer wealth of visual data, the painstaking chronicle of changes in dress, transport, street layouts, buildings, housing and landscape that captivates us so much today, offering us a powerful link with the past and with the lives of our ancestors.

Computers have now made it possible for Frith's many thousands of images to be accessed almost instantly. The archive offers every one of us an opportunity to examine the places where we and our families have lived and worked down the years. Its images, depicting our shared past, are now bringing pleasure and enlightenment to millions around the world a century and more after his death.

For further information visit: www.francisfrith.com

INTERIOR DECORATION

Frith's photographs can be seen framed and as giant wall murals in thousands of pubs, restaurants, hotels, banks, retail stores and other public buildings throughout Britain. These provide interesting and attractive décor, generating strong local interest and acting as a powerful reminder of gentler days in our increasingly busy and frenetic world.

FRITH PRODUCTS

All Frith photographs are available as prints and posters in a variety of different sizes and styles. In the UK we also offer a range of other gift and stationery products illustrated with Frith photographs, although many of these are not available for delivery outside the UK – see our web site for more information on the products available for delivery in your country.

THE INTERNET

Over 100,000 photographs of Britain can be viewed and purchased on the Frith web site. The web site also includes memories and reminiscences contributed by our customers, who have personal knowledge of localities and of the people and properties depicted in Frith photographs. If you wish to learn more about a specific town or village you may find these reminiscences fascinating to browse. Why not add your own comments if you think they would be of interest to others? See **www.francisfrith.com**

PLEASE HELP US BRING FRITH'S PHOTOGRAPHS TO LIFE

Our authors do their best to recount the history of the places they write about. They give insights into how particular towns and villages developed, they describe the architecture of streets and buildings, and they discuss the lives of famous people who lived there. But however knowledgeable our authors are, the story they tell is necessarily incomplete.

Frith's photographs are so much more than plain historical documents. They are living proofs of the flow of human life down the generations. They show real people at real moments in history; and each of those people is the son or daughter of someone, the brother or sister, aunt or uncle, grandfather or grandmother of someone else. All of them lived, worked and played in the streets depicted in Frith's photographs.

We would be grateful if you would give us your insights into the places shown in our photographs: the streets and buildings, the shops, businesses and industries. Post your memories of life in those streets on the Frith website: what it was like growing up there, who ran the local shop and what shopping was like years ago; if your workplace is shown tell us about your working day and what the building is used for now. Read other visitors' memories and reconnect with your shared local history and heritage. With your help more and more Frith photographs can be brought to life, and vital memories preserved for posterity, and for the benefit of historians in the future.

Wherever possible, we will try to include some of your comments in future editions of our books. Moreover, if you spot errors in dates, titles or other facts, please let us know, because our archive records are not always completely accurate—they rely on 140 years of human endeavour and hand-compiled records. You can email us using the contact form on the website.

Thank you!

For further information, trade, or author enquiries
please contact us at the address below:

**The Francis Frith Collection, Oakley Business Park,
Wylye Road, Dinton, Wiltshire SP3 5EU England.**
Tel: +44 (0)1722 716 376 Fax: +44 (0)1722 716 881
e-mail: sales@francisfrith.co.uk **www.francisfrith.com**